JUST OUT

OF REACH

Just Out of Reach

JUST OUT OF REACH

LAUREN-BROOKS WILSON

Cover Photo by
LAUREN-BROOKS WILSON

Just Out of Reach

Lauren-Brooks Wilson

This book is dedicated to:

The memories of all the kids.

Just Out of Reach

Disclaimer:

Characters have been combined and events have been condensed. These are my memories; I am the teller of my own story. To protect the privacy and identity of others, names have been changed.

Just Out of Reach

Lauren-Brooks Wilson

Contents

CHAPTER ONE 11

CHAPTER TWO 31

CHAPTER THREE 43

CHAPTER FOUR 57

CHAPTER FIVE 67

CHAPTER SIX 81

Just Out of Reach

CHAPTER ONE

Number: 1
Here We Go

When I was six, my family got our first foster kid, Angie. The day I learned the news all of my feelings were intertwined. I was anxious, confused, and wondering what I was going to do with her. She was 5 years old. I remember seeing her for the first time, her long pale blond hair (it was down to her lower back), very pale skin, her beautiful blue eyes, her polka-dot shirt and blue jeans. Her smile was crooked; it showed that she didn't know what would happen next. When we arrived at the home to meet her, Angie was standing on her bed in the corner of the room that she shared with some of the other children she had been living with. Such a strange situation when you go to meet the person who you hope will one day become your sister. Once we got in the car my story began.

She and I were fast best friends. Like sisters from the start. Since Angie's dad had gone to jail and her mom was using drugs, they were not doing the stuff to get her back out of foster care. The state talked to my parents about caring for her and keeping her to adopt. She'd been living with some family members for a while but they couldn't keep her forever. It didn't bother me that I wasn't included in the conversations about her staying because she would be my sister forever; exactly what I wanted.

We treated Angie like our own kid from the beginning. That's because no one really cared more about her than we did. Our family would go ice skating at the community skate arena. We loved to go on our favorite night, Friday. That was our favorite time to be there because on Friday nights at 9:00pm they would turn out the bright lights and turn on the colorful lights. We would skate to the old 80's

& 90's songs under the colored lights until Mom made us take off the skates before we collapsed from exhaustion or hurt ourselves. We would have so much fun. Mom taught me how to skate when I was 3 and as soon as Angie moved in she was teaching her too. Angie was a little slow to learn at first, but once she got the hang of it she and I were off. We spent hours trying to figure out how to spin around in circles in the big colored spots on the ice. Falling never seemed to bother us. We would just help each other up again and again. We pretended we were professional ice skaters, laughing, holding hands and dreaming of all the wonderful tricks we could do.

I have this friend who is more like a brother, Oliver, who I have known since I was two. Once Angie came the three of us became like the Three Musketeers. You couldn't separate us. People always say that whenever three kids are together there is always one being left out, not us. We stuck together like glue. For Halloween that year Angie and I dressed up as Lollipop Kids from the Wizard of OZ and Oliver was a spy. We looked awesome and spent hours out trick-or-treating. In our home Angie got a brother too, just three single kids together making a family. We were inseparable, playing hour after hour in the garden, neighborhood and going on adventures.

When the Disney movie Camp Rock premiered on TV, Angie and I were ready. Months of commercials and a final channel count down had overwhelmed us with excitement. We were driving Mom crazy with questions about how much longer. Mom came up with this great plan to get us out of the house. Plus, unknown to me at the time, we didn't have cable and couldn't see the movie at our home. So to solve the problem of our excitement and the fact we couldn't see it at home Mom planned this "Camp Rock Party" at Grandma's. We even made signs to cheer on the actors on the screen and clapped, sang along and danced as we watched together. We stayed at Grandma's house with Mom as a sleep over party sharing the futon and sleeping with our gigantic stuffed animals. We loved Camp Rock weekend. It became one of our favorite movies of all time. Once it was available on video we watched it all the time singing along to the songs and dancing about together in front of the TV. Each one of these memories being created daily only reinforced that I knew we were supposed to be together. So did my parents.

Lauren-Brooks Wilson

    For Mother's day my mother and grandmother planned a trip for us four girls to go to Hawaii. Angie and I were so excited! The plan was for us to stay with our grandma's friends who lived there. The state had to give permission for us to take Angie with us. I thought that was weird because by this time I considered her ours even though it had been only five months. The social worker was slow in getting back with mom and dad about the permission and it almost wrecked the trip. Although the social worker said it was fine for her to go, because she had another mom and dad they also had to agree. BUT her father said no, and they couldn't find her mom. So the social worker went to court and got an order from the judge saying she could come with us. I couldn't understand why her mom didn't want to know what she was doing and how great her life was, and I especially didn't understand why her dad would want her to stay home instead of go. If she hadn't been there, I would have been very sad because we did everything together.

    Finally, with the permission to go sorted out, the packing and preparation time nearly drove us crazy; we just wanted to go. Suitcases and backpacks in hand we headed to the airport and Angie took her first plane ride with us. Once we arrived Mom kind of freaked out with worry over sun burns. Sunscreen was critical. So every morning we would strip down to our undies and our mom would slather us in sun screen from the tip of our ears to the bottoms of our feet. The best part about it was that both Angie and I were super ticklish. So it always felt like we were having a tickle-fest to start off the day.

On our first outing, while walking to the white beach we found this huge spider. It was about eight inches tall and about five inches wide. The colors on it were black and yellow. A spiky looking line ran all the way down its back. Angie and I both started to shriek with terror and caused such a fuss that Mom and Grandma thought someone was dying. We were so grossed out and immediately thought that these spiders were everywhere and refused to calm down. We watched every step and peered around all corners for over an hour until we forgot about it and moved on to the fun of picking coral to take home.

Lauren-Brooks Wilson

    To make sure that we had a full Hawaii experience Mom and Grandma planned for us to go to a Hawaiian Luau. They put on this great show of dancing, tricks and cooking the pig while it was underground. The problem was that on our day it started to rain. This great area outside on the ocean that was all set up for us to eat and see this show was soaked, and so were we. The owners wanted the guest to have a good time anyway and not waste the food, so we moved the party inside the hotel nearby. The room was just a large hall. Neither Angie nor I liked much of the food, but we sure did like the dancing. Even inside a man twirled fire sticks and showed off amazing tricks. During dessert a nice lady named Andréa called all the children up to the stage and gave us hula skirts. She taught us a cool Hawaiian dance that we performed for every one of the people at the luau.

    Breakfast time each morning was a planning time for the next adventure. There was so much to do and we wanted to see and experience as much as we could. I had been to Hawaii with Mom and Dad when I was five but wanted to share everything I could with my new sister.

Just Out of Reach

A day later we were at the beach snorkeling. My mom and I were off to the reef with our snorkels about five feet away from my grandma who was wandering around in the water with Angie until it was her turn to go snorkeling. Because she had never done anything like that before, Mom spent time back home teaching her to swim and how to use the snorkel mask and breather. At one point we turned around to wave to them when my grandma stepped on a rock. At least that's what it looked like, but it wasn't a rock. It was a huge turtle! Angie and I were so shocked and in awe of the size we wondered for weeks about how old it might have been. After Mom and I came back from snorkeling she took Angie out to go see the reef and all the fish. We saw all sorts of fish. The clown fish, and some huge fish about the same size as me when I was six, so about four feet long. We also saw fish as small as an infant's pinkie finger.

Volcanos, beaches, water falls, ice cream, gigantic plants, made every day an adventure and every adventure brought us closer together. We all had so much fun on that trip. Neither of us would ever forget it.

Lauren-Brooks Wilson

Although I was in the first grade, Angie was not ready for school yet. I could tell that something was not right when she first came since she was five and didn't know her alphabet or any of the children's songs or shows that I did. Down the street from our house was Patti's home. She was a lady who had three grown children, and a husband and her house was a daycare. I had been going there ever since I was 18 months old. I love Patty and wanted Angie to have the same love and care that I got growing up. Mom and Dad asked if Angie could go there.

Patti said, "Of course".

I was so happy to share my special safe home with her and even happier that I would get to see her each day after the bus dropped me off from school. She fit in well with the other kids and Patti spent time teaching her things she needed to know to be ready for school in the fall the next year. When I got there in the afternoon, we would play inside together, eat together, play outside together. We would do everything together. It was such a safe place to be when our parents were at work. By the time school started she was so smart for a Kindergartener she probably could have gone straight to first grade. She was so kind and such a good friend to everyone.

There were so many things that Angie didn't know about or how to do when she came to live with us. She seemed so confused about everything at the beginning, but was such a nice kid that she wanted to learn everything. My mom and dad spent a lot of time teaching her basic things that most five-year olds would know like brushing your teeth or picking out your clothes, taking a bath and washing yourself. But she also had not learned other things either like swimming, bike riding, singing songs and how to eat as a family. I taught her how to use her imagination. It was important that I had a job too because when you have a kid who comes and needs so much attention it can leave you feeling useless, unless someone notices your strengths and asks you to help too.

Later that year, in the summer, we traveled when we could get time to Eastern Washington. We stayed at our extended family share home. We would hang out day after day at the pool in the community center. We would play

Lauren-Brooks Wilson

Marco Polo, tag, practice underwater somersaults, and see who could stay the longest under water. I always won but Angie never minded because she just wanted to be together. When we would visit that house, it was extra special because Auntie, Uncle and Cousin Connor would join us and we would be an even more complete family than ever. Those times were fun.

    As the months went on and summer turned to fall it was time to prepare for school. Angie had grown up so much over the time she had lived with us. But it wasn't always easy. Sometimes Angie would just stare into space. Who knows why? She would just kind of disappear. My mom would sit with her and try to talk with her, but she was never able to say what she was thinking. Me being only six years old, made it confusing. My questions seemed like they would be easy to get an answer to. "Why does she just sit there not doing anything?" But it always seemed that no one had an answer for me. I never understood why. It sometimes scared me. Most of the time she was so cheery and happy with her goofy smile.

Just Out of Reach

Angie and I shared a room and in the mornings were the worst, before everyone woke up. I would hear Mom come in and find her. No one ever knew how long she would have been awake, just staring blankly at ... nothing. It took so long for her to get away from the times when she just sat there with a blank expression. It looked like she wasn't thinking of anything and if it were possible she wasn't even on earth. It was clear to me that the longer she was with us as part of our family the less she seemed to drift away into that emptiness. She was healing. We were good together; all of us needed each other.

As much as we were a family there was a continual reminder that she wasn't part of us. When you have a foster kid in your home there are always people coming to meet with them. Most of the time they just wanted to talk to Angie, Mom and Dad and mostly just ignored me. There was one case manager, Patricia, who came to visit us; she always made time for me. I had to learn that the state social worker's job is to visit the foster kids, make plans for their life and make sure they were safe. Patricia wasn't a state social worker but she was another person to keep an eye on the situation. She always made time for me and to ask me what I felt about Angie in my home, about my feelings. To the others I didn't matter but this worker made it feel like I was part of the process too. I don't remember all the things I told her or what I felt most of the time but I remember one thing, I enjoyed her asking me. I remember telling everyone that took the time to ask me that Angie was like a sister. Well, she was a sister; just not a biological sister, and even at six years old I knew that wasn't the most important thing.

She meant so much to me. In all honesty, there were times where I felt like I wasn't getting enough attention. But that rarely happened and I guess made our time more real because isn't that like it is with families who have lots of kids? The attention has to get spread out. I always loved her and can't even remember a time when we fought.

Since Angie had been away from her parents care for more than a year there was a big meeting about permanency and Angie staying with us forever. For some reason some relatives showed up at the meeting which took place at the beginning of November. For the most part Angie had one social worker but then at the end she had three new ones all with different supervisors. So because they had changed so much another meeting had to be held at the beginning of December. Angie and I were not invited to these meetings even though what they talked about would affect us forever. After the first meeting, Angie wrote a letter to the social worker and judge who was part of her case telling them what she wanted, just in case someone wanted to know. Here's how it went.

> "Dear Judge,
>
> I want to live with my dad but if he can't make good choices then I want to live with my mom. If she can't stop using drugs and I can't live with her then I want to stay right where I am. This is my family, mommy Sheila, daddy Steven, and my big sister, Lauren. I don't want to move to another stranger's home, even if they are family.
>
> Thank you,
>
> Angie."

My mom made sure that this letter got to the judge. It is a weird thing to think that a person's entire life can be changed by some stranger's opinion about relationships and what they are worth.

This second meeting was awful... My mother and father attended because the new social worked decided it was necessary to consider moving Angie to this new relative's home. The way the social worker decided to determine where Angie would live would be by vote. The choices were us or those distant relatives. The distant relatives won because there were more of them at the table to vote than my mom and dad. I have learned that once the Department social workers make up their mind (even if they are the sixth one in a year) there is no changing it. Angie's letter meant nothing. The decision was made and so the calendars came out and a plan for her to leave by the end of the month was made. I guess even though we had a whole year it meant nothing. She had to move on the 27th of December, just two days after Christmas.

As part of the "transition plan" Angie's new family invited her out to go putt-putt golfing with them. She didn't want to go alone so Mom and I went along. What a strange situation: the two families getting together looking from the outside like old friends when in truth we were on opposite sides. We loved and wanted to keep Angie and they were coming to steal her from our lives. I don't know how we got through that month. Angie did not want to leave our family and she certainly didn't want to live with another set of strangers, even if someone said she was related. She wrote another letter to the court stating she didn't want to leave. The court didn't care. We lost her.

There was so much sadness in the house but my mom tried so hard to help Angie accept that it had to be this way, even though she ached for it to be different. I hated all the preparation for her to go because I didn't want it to happen. Packing, collecting, organizing, boxes of adventures, gifts, clothes, memories connected to every item. Mom spent hours going through our photos and organizing them into a memory book. I didn't understand why there was no fight; our family was so powerless to the decisions of these people who had never even met me and Angie.

Lauren-Brooks Wilson

To help me say goodbye, Mom and I made a plan. We decided that since she would be with us for Christmas and then going to a new home she might need something homemade and full of our love to take with her. The perfect solution was to make a blanket for her; the kind of blanket made of polar fleece and tied together all around the sides. Mom and I went to the fabric store to go get our fabric and that's when reality of everything that was happening to our family and Angie really sunk in. I realized that she really was really leaving and we couldn't do anything about it. I curled up on the tiled floor of the fabric store and cried. No one could stop me. A flood of this crazy reality hit me and the sadness over whelmed me. I would never be whole if she really left. But all I could do was learn to accept that the Department had made up their mind and what I could control was making sure that Angie knew that I would never forget her. After two hours of crying and talking while sitting on the floor in the isle at the store, Mom and I left to go home. Dad and Angie had a two night sleep over at my Dad's mom's house, my Oma's. That way Mom and I could build the blanket in secret and get it wrapped. There was lots of crying during the construction of that blanket but in the end it was perfect.

Just Out of Reach

We took our time decorating for Christmas that year, trying to keep every memory and moment. Mom sorted out all of Angie's things in boxes in the basement and I wrapped her blanket up for her as a Christmas present. I have never said goodbye to anyone so dear to my heart before and could not have been prepared, ever.

On her last night with us Oliver's mom gave us three musketeers, stuffed animals to help us always remember. Oliver got a lion. I got a pig and named it Pinky because that was her nickname in our home. Whenever it was time to hold hands she always grabbed Mom's pinky. Angie got two elephant stuffy's; one named Oliver, the other one named Lauren. The three of us had been reduced to no more than just stuffed animals representing what we had together.

On the 27th of December Angie's new family took her and drove away with the promise that I could write to her and we could be connected through our words. For months I wrote letters and sent them to her; that dumb family just sent them right back. The social worker and family lied and had only told me what they thought I wanted to hear to make me feel better at the moment. Really what they told me was to make them feel better about taking my sister from me. Telling a lie to a kid is a selfish and cowardly move by the adults. But that wasn't enough for them. After a few weeks a DSHS person showed up at our door to ask a bunch of questions about how we cared for Angie. The other family had called them and lied to them saying that we had abused, starved and called her fat. None of these lies were true and the process of being investigated when we had loved Angie so much was just piling on the hurt to our family.

I still miss her; she meant so much to me. I loved her and I still do. Each night since that sad day in December so many years ago, I fall to sleep with my little piece of Angie close to my heart.

Just Out of Reach

CHAPTER TWO

Number: 2
Strong Enough to Try Again

    Well, when your heart breaks into as many pieces as our family heart did it is really hard to think about doing it again. We took five months to get to a place where we could think about having another child come to our home without disrespecting the memories and plans we had made with Angie. In May we all agreed we could try again but we didn't want to have another girl because we thought it would feel like we were replacing Angie; none of us wanted that. She was too special. So we decided to ask to have a boy placed in our home. That was exciting to me because I had wanted a brother and a sister and didn't really care what order I got them.

It didn't take long before Mom and Dad were called about a two year old who needed a home, and his mom and dad wanted to relinquish. This was a big word for signing away your rights as a parent so the kid can be adopted, but what it meant to me was that the mom and dad no longer wanted their kid. This was a strange concept for me because I couldn't understand why parents would do that. So the Department likes to do things their way and their way involves having more meetings. To start the process of getting my brother, Mom and Dad went to a meeting, without me and met Cooper. His social worker and parents were there too. I guess the care provider who had him was there, but I can't really tell why she was invited since she was giving him back. Mom and Dad learned that Cooper had been away from his family for a long time. Almost since the day he was born it seemed like someone else had been caring for him and now he was two and half years old. We learned that he had lived in 12 homes and was the middle son with an older and younger brother. None of them had lived together and the other two boys had families who wanted to keep them, but none of them wanted Cooper to live with them. Mom and Dad came back from the meeting and made the decision that we could have him come to our home. One call to the social worker and a "transition plan" to help him adjust from his previous home to ours with some visits and then sleep over long visits and then he would move in. The plan was to take about a month for us to get to know him and move him completely. BUT the care provider called just two nights after the meeting saying she couldn't take it any longer and he had to move the next day. Mom kind of panicked. You see she is a planner and this was going fast. All of a sudden we were going to get another kid, a boy, a little boy. We had never had a boy. There was a lot of excitement that next day, and Mom was running around trying to get ready for a two year old: potty seats, bed rails, high chair, and what about daycare?

The social worker didn't come but the foster mother who was giving him to us brought him. I got to be home with Mom when they arrived. Mom didn't want to overwhelm him with too many people when he first got here. He was so small, just about the smallest two year old I had ever seen. But don't let his size fool you. That kid could talk, run, throw balls, and come up with the craziest things. After he settled in, and I got used to the naps and diapers and little boy toys all around, I liked him. He still wore onesies and had a pacifier! I really grew to love him and the more he stayed, the less alone I felt.

Our house was under a remodel when he moved in and because of "foster care rules" he and I couldn't sleep in the same room because I was seven and he was two and we were not the same gender. That meant that I had to share my mom and dad's temporary bedroom in the dining room and sleep on a cot until the rest of the remodel was done. It got really crowded which was frustrating at times. Parts of it I didn't mind too much because I like to sleep in the same room as my parents, but it did seem like a useless rule. I think the Department has lots of those.

Because Cooper was so young he went to daycare instead of school. That meant that Mom and Dad had to go more places to pick us up. Since Patti didn't do daycare anymore at her home, he went to a really nice place that Mom found that first night. The director liked our family and rather than putting him on a wait list let him come right away. There were two things that you should know about Cooper. One, he was super small and two, he was super smart. He learned things so fast. After about two months at our home mom figured he was ready to stop wearing diapers and in only two days he was potty trained. (Mom used M&M's to bribe him and it worked.) He could also take things apart and put them back together and he was really good at puzzles. We played in the back yard a lot and climbed on the playground together. He was a good aim with a football and baseball too. It just seemed like everything he did he was really good at. He had the prettiest blue eyes and brown hair cut to look like a college boy. I let myself love him.

After he had lived with us for about six months things started to change. The social worker decided that he should have visits with his real mom and dad even though they hadn't been happening at all and the plan was for him to be my brother forever. Once the visits started then things got really hard at home. He started acting weird to my mom and dad, glaring at Dad whenever he was near Mom and always trying to draw the attention to him. Mom said that it was because he thought he needed to protect her from Dad because he had seen dads hurt moms before. When we started to see this, Mom called the social worker and tried to get some help from a counselor for him and our family. They ignored her calls. When she did finally get to talk to them they thought it was not true. That what we were seeing was false. They said we would be fine, but we were not fine. It seemed like the more times he saw his biological family, the more crazy his actions would be. He started to do things that scared Mom and Dad, like saying things in front of other people that were not true about us. That meant that a lot of times I had to be around to be a "witness" if he ever made a claim against us for doing something. It was a weird situation to be in because we wanted this to work for everyone so badly. I mean how many times can a little kid be moved before they are messed up forever? We were already home number thirteen in two years!

Things were tough. Mom and Dad were arguing more about what to do. The social worker was not helping or even coming to the home to see us. It got really bad when Cooper started to get kicked out of daycare for being dangerous to the other kids. One day he took a cup of water from the bathroom and poured it in the heater in the sleeping room during nap time nearly causing a fire. He started to push and hit other kids and the daycare director was going to kick him out. Mom was trying to work, so she had Grandma go to the daycare and stay with him all day. That worked for a little bit but then at the same time it was getting harder at home. He was sneaking around the house at night and taking things; he even opened the front door in the middle of the night. Mom said that if we couldn't keep him safe in our home and if the Department wouldn't give us help to learn other ways to support him and help him ourselves we would have to have him move. I was torn apart when I finally learned that was a possibility. I really loved him and wanted Cooper to be my baby brother, but at the same time having him in our family was causing so much drama and chaos all the time. I didn't know what to do to help make things better and I sure didn't want things to get any worse. It seemed like no one could help us and even though my mom knows a lot about kids and what they need, she couldn't solve this problem and make our family whole. I felt like my heart was going to be pulled apart again. I couldn't let that happen, but I was powerless.

We made it through Christmas and seven months after Mom started asking for help for our family the social worker finally hired a therapist. She came to the house a few times and then determined that we were all making it up and that Mom and Dad needed to have better parenting skills. WHAT!!! My mom and dad had great parenting skills; Cooper was just always putting on a show of good behavior when she was there. It was like he knew how to make someone look crazy, but he was only three by then. How could that be? So Mom and Dad asked that the therapist not come back anymore and we were on our own again.

By February Mom and Dad decided, with a lot of arguing and talking and writing lists and every other way to come to a conclusion, that we as a family could not be Cooper's family. It was crushing….. to have lost the first two siblings that I ever had a chance to have. By this time I had a pretty good idea about what I thought of the DSHS foster care and adoption system.

Lauren-Brooks Wilson

So here we are again, making a photo album of the time he lived with us, packing up all his belongings and having meetings (that I still wasn't invited to attend) to prepare to have him move, again. I know that Mom was heartbroken and I tried my best to be really good and help whenever I could, but it was hard for me too. It wasn't the same as when Angie left because she was MY sister and we did so much together. Cooper was my little brother, but it was just different from the beginning. Our family was being ripped apart because of the decision. Something had to change.

The social worker found a gay couple who lived in a nearby town who wanted to have Cooper. The idea was that if Cooper was adopted by them then he might not have such a hard time because there would be no "mom" to be beaten up just two dads. Because they were gay and had a small family, they said they wanted us to stay in their lives as extended family members, Mom like an aunt, me like a cousin, and grandma as, well, the grandma. So with this plan in place the family was approved and he moved. Mom told them all about his favorites and explained his bedtime routines and how he liked to read books when he woke up and went to bed. *Goodnight Moon* was his favorite but he also really liked giraffes, the color orange, and *Curious George*. We had gotten video and photos from when he was a newborn and baby from people who had cared for him before us and put it all together in the photo book. We wanted him to have his history and know that people loved him when he was little.

To keep the move less "official", Mom took all his stuff and Cooper to his new family on February 12th. But this didn't feel like a goodbye since we would be seeing each other soon. We had plans to go ice skating, swimming, and have play times. Grandma was going to have us both over for special sleep over in a few months after he got settled. It all seemed fine until Mom called to try to set up some time together. They hung up on her. See, they lied too. They didn't want us to stay involved; they just wanted to get Cooper. All the talk of us being like cousins and getting together to go ice skating or play at our favorite parks and beaches was just lies. I never got to see my little brother again and he never saw us either. Mom told me later that that family turned out to be a bad family that hurt him. The

Lauren-Brooks Wilson

Department had to find him another home. Over two years later Mom learned that home number fifteen got to adopt him. My memories and feelings of Cooper are mixed because we tried so hard and were honest with what we needed, but just couldn't seem to make it work. Ultimately we had to make a decision to save our existing family, but the sadness about him having to go with two more families and suffer abuse and confusion will always be in our minds. He was so smart and he learned so much during the year he lived with us. I often wonder what does he remember now? Does he feel abandoned by us or did someone tell him how much we loved him? I will never know.

Just Out of Reach

CHAPTER THREE

Numbers: 3 & 4
This Should Work

Our hearts were broken and we didn't want to have our hearts broken again, so we decided that we would take in a child who was definitely going to go back home. That way we couldn't and wouldn't get too attached. Kylee was our solution. She was a young Vietnamese teen whose mom lived near our house and the plan was for her to reunite (that's the big word the social workers use) with her mom by the time school started next fall. She came to us on June 22. She was a "sweet" thirteen year old girl who went to middle school. The problem with saying yes to Kylee was that her room wasn't finished because of all the construction. In fact it was the "home base" for all the construction and in the worst shape than any of the rooms in the house. We had three days to make it livable. Dad had planned a fishing trip that weekend so he was gone, but Mom and I worked together. We cleared, cleaned, painted, bought a bed and got carpet installed. When Dad came home, he helped get the rest of the furniture and put in the lights, switches and trim. Grandma even came down to make curtains. The room was beautiful when her social worker brought her home. Later in her stay with us she did a report in school where the kids were supposed to talk about their "heaven". She wrote about her bedroom.

Kylee's family was from Vietnam so she would talk in Vietnamese on the phone with her mom and siblings. She had eight brothers and sisters (mostly sisters). Vietnamese is a language with a lot of sounds that I had never heard before so when she would talk we would all listen in. She also liked to cook, so Mom would help her shop and make Vietnamese dinner for the family. These were not my favorite meals because I'm picky eater, but I did learn to like a few things.

Lauren-Brooks Wilson

For only being thirteen years old she sure knew a lot about cooking and taking care of kids.

Then sort of out of the blue a social worker called and said that this little boy only four years old needed a "forever home". Chris came two days after Kylee on June 24th. Taking two kids in two days who are so different in age and have such different plans was not the smartest idea when we look back on it, but in the moment we thought we were doing the right thing.

I wasn't home when Chris showed up, but when I got there he was sitting on the counter crying. That seemed to go on nearly the whole time he lived with us. I thought he was a cry baby and never really liked him. He demanded what he wanted and didn't show any respect for how hard our family was trying. I learned later why he was so upset that first day. He used to live in the forest with his grandparents in a trailer. His parents were still stuck in a bad cycle of using drugs and violence. It seems like he had seen a lot of those fights because when he didn't get his way he could really get scary. His grandparents were tired of the family mess and decided

Just Out of Reach

that they were too old to raise a little boy like Chris. His "Papa" drove him to our house to live, but no one told Chris that the plan was for him to stay forever. It was the social worker's job but she didn't do it. She didn't even show up at our home on the day he came. When his "Papa" drove away he flipped out. Because no one had explained to him about foster care or what his future might look like, he was really confused about everything and it all came out as anger.

Chris was a boy who did what he wanted. Although he was only four years old, he was really strong from spending a lot of time alone in the forest with his grandparents. He wanted to eat meat at every meal and told my mom that he would only drink "pink milk". I think that meant strawberry flavored milk. Well, that didn't go over so well with my mom because she is big into eating healthy. It was kind of funny to hear him wake up and first thing ask, "Are we eating meat today?" Don't get me wrong… we're not vegetarian and usually eat meat every day, but the way he asked was so direct it was as if he was pure carnivore. He was always so happy when Mom said, "Yes, we are".

Lauren-Brooks Wilson

When we unpacked the belongings his grandpa had brought, he had a lot of things that didn't fit and were the wrong kind of clothes for summer. That happens a lot with foster kids. They come to your house and need so much just to get caught up with the basic things everyone should have like pants, pajamas, socks, and swim suits. It can feel kind of unfair when they come because your parents go out shopping and the grandparents buy them toys to welcome them. Since my mom and dad took time to explain this then, in my mind I could understand the need. But I am just a kid, and with all the other attention from the kids who came it was easy to feel jealous at times.

Suddenly with these two new kids summer just seemed to happen. I was eight years old now, I had just finished second grade, and here we were with our third and fourth foster kids. Because Grandma was not working anymore, she became our summertime daycare provider. It would have been, and should have been a great summer, full of day adventures, crafts, mini-trips and imagination. That's the way it always had been between me and Grandma. It became clear very quickly that I was not going to have that time. Kylee was a totally different person when Mom and Dad weren't around. Grandma tried to explain it to them but no one believed her or me. It made me sad at first and then mad at the way she treated Grandma when we would leave to do something each day. She moped and took way too long to get ready; making us late for everything grandma had planned all summer long. It really bugged me because she was only this way when we were with Grandma. She was a totally nice and cool person when Mom and Dad were home. It seemed like I was the only one who ever got to see this mean side of her other than Grandma who thought she was like that all the time. It didn't make sense why she needed to do that or change for different people. I just kept remembering that she would be going home by the end of the summer. So I figured I would just deal the best I could and tried to enjoy the trips we did get to do like the zoo, aquarium, beaches and parks.

Because our family was growing we needed to buy a bigger car to handle the family size and trips we liked to go on. Dad did the research and we all got to go to the car dealer to pick out the new seven seat S.U.V. with three rows. We climbed all throughout and pushed every button to see what it did. Now that we had the new SUV it seemed to make sense to take a week long summer vacation to the Oregon Coast to camp and ride ATV's. Like a family, we brought Kylee, Chris, and Opa (my grandfather). Other foster families put their foster kids into respite homes which are like babysitting homes, when they do family activities and trips, but not us. If you live in our family, you are one of us and are invited to do everything. The social workers for both the kids had to get permission from their parents to leave the state and ride the ATV's. But unlike Angie's, these social workers got everyone to say yes quickly.

On the car ride there everything was good. It was long, but we had stuff to do and were excited to see where we would end up. At the end of the six hour drive we worked together to set up the tents and make our campsite ours. It was fun and we got to ride our bikes around the campground. Chris kept asking where we were going to sleep and it seemed pretty obvious to me that we were sleeping in tents since we were going camping and had already set them up. He asked so many times all through the ride there and right up to bedtime. Each time he asked someone we would say in the

Just Out of Reach

tent, but I guess that didn't mean anything to him. I was confused because I was told he lived in the forest before he lived with us so what was the problem? Well, as it turned out he had never slept in a tent before because he had always lived in a trailer. Funny how we think about things. We know and think others understand it the way we do, but not always. Because there were so many of us and foster care rules about who could sleep together I was in a tent with Dad. Mom, Kylee and Chris had another, while Opa got his own.

We went ATV riding on this gigantic sandy hill and over the dunes to the ocean. Dad took us all go-cart racing, Opa took us to the Sea Lion Caves on the coast, and we had a really good time. Chris got in some trouble for trying to drive the ATV too fast, but I couldn't blame him for trying because it is so much fun. We even celebrated his fifth birthday with a pizza party and gave him presents that Mom brought along. Then came the drive home...... it was horrible. That day was the worst day to be with Chris. I had to sit with him in the very back of the car, when all of the grown-ups were way up in the front; so much for the awesomeness of the three rows. He was having a temper tantrum because when we stopped at a rest stop my mom pleaded with Chris NOT to pee on the toilet seat. This was something that he had been doing since he moved in and continued to do no matter what Mom tried to get him to stop. Well, he did anyway and he got caught. He started crying really hard and he never stopped. He went on and on and on and on and on until we got home, but he still cried in his room having a temper tantrum. It annoyed me so much. It probably annoyed me the most because I had to sit next to the snot flying, crazy crying, cranky five year old boy who had just peed all over a toilet seat. Gross.

To try to help him adjust and understand that his grandparents still loved him and that he could see them, my mom and I drove with Chris to Eastern Washington a week after we got back from Oregon to celebrate his birthday and to visit with his grandparents in the woods. I was nervous about another road trip but this one was a nice trip because Chris was so excited to see them. In between these visits he got to call them on the phone but the cell service was so bad in the woods the calls couldn't happen that much. They gave him a fishing pole. My dad fishes so they thought he and Chris could go together. It was really hard for him to say goodbye when it was time to go. I guess that makes sense because they had cared for him for so long before he came to us. But eventually we had to get him in the car and drive away. It was hard to see him so sad on the three-hour drive home. There was so much uncertainty in his life. I can't imagine what I would do if someone dropped me off and told me I couldn't live with the people I had loved for my lifetime. As much as his behaviors bothered me and disrupted my life, every day I was sad for him.

The whole time Chris lived with us he stayed the same, annoying, rude, and happy every once in a while, little kid. He had visits with his mom sometimes, and it seemed like he just really wanted her and his dad to be nice to each other so he could go home. What that meant was when he would come home from his visits he would be especially cranky and hard to be around until he "transitioned" back into his thinking that he lived here. It seemed like he was just going along with our rules until he could get out and go home so that meant he didn't really like us at all. The problem was the Department wasn't going to send him home, but no one was taking time to help him understand that or tell him what was going on.

One Sunday night in August Chris got mad. The reason was... well there really wasn't a reason that he could say. He had just come home from a visit with his parents and just got super mad. My mom had him go to his room the way we always did to settle back in, but this time was not like the rest. He started punching at the walls to see if he could get through them and to antagonize my parents and the rest of the family. After Chris was in his room and my mom had the alarm on Chris's bedroom door on, we thought he would settle down. The alarm was necessary because otherwise he would sneak out at night and everyone was afraid he might try to run away and find his grandparents. Other times when he was in time out it would be turned on to help him stay in his room during his time out. Well this time he opened that door and the alarm went off. With the alarm blaring Chris came stomping out the door. His face was horrible. It was scary for a five year old, and it scared **_me,_** the eight year old. It probably scared me because lots of things were going on. Chris went crazy. He threatened to kill me and was running at me and swinging to hit Mom. She sat down with him in front of her holding his arms and legs to get him to calm down. Mom used to work at the hospital with kids who had lots of problems but I had never seen her have to hold a kid before to be safe. After about an hour he finally quieted down and Mom wanted to let him go but he would not agree to be safe. That's the term my mom kept saying. He needed to be safe with his body and to other people and things. He was so stubborn he wouldn't agree. Because he wasn't swinging at anyone anymore, Mom let him go, and he immediately got up and tried to throw a lamp at her. Dad came in just in time to catch the bookshelf from falling on Mom that Chris had pulled away from the wall. Dad held him down on his bed with his blanket because he was throwing things, trying to knock things over on top of my parents. While my dad was holding Chris down safe, he needed a witness to make sure he wasn't hurting him, so Kylee stayed. See when you are a foster parent there are a lot of rules about how to discipline a kid in your home, but there are not any books to tell someone how to protect your family from a violent five year old.

Lauren-Brooks Wilson

    To give some space to everyone for a bit, Mom and I left. I had a complete melt down in the car. I was scared to go back home so Mom called up the neighbors across the street and asked them if I could go there until this was over. Thankfully they said yes. So I went to their house until about 10:00pm. Mom also called all the people on his case, including the emergency social worker line because it was Sunday and the regular worker wasn't in. When I came home, lots of things had happened. The police and DSHS social worker were at my house. Chris had finally calmed down, but if one person did something wrong he would flame up again. Thankfully, the emergency social worker took him out of our house; Chris left us that night. Unlike the tough decisions about Angie and Cooper, with Chris it was easy to see that after that night it was too dangerous and caused too much stress to keep him at our house. I never saw him again and didn't really want to. I hope he found someplace where he could live and learn to understand what happened to his family.

    We were back to just Kylee.

Just Out of Reach

Lauren-Brooks Wilson

CHAPTER FOUR

Numbers: 3 & 5
Maybe We Will Get It Right

Between Chris and his explosions and Kylee being so mean to my grandma, my summer was kind of ruined. See, Chris left in August, even though the plan was for Chris to stay. Kylee was supposed to leave before school started; that didn't happen. The delay for Kylee's move was because the social workers changed a few time. This happens a lot with the Department. It seemed that even though we knew the plan for her and helped with all the visitations, the new social workers took forever to catch on. She stayed well after the school year started.

Just Out of Reach

Since Chris had left and we knew that Kylee would be going soon, we sort of started, "shopping" again for another kid. This time my mom and dad said we would only bring a kid into our home who was really available to be adopted. I was getting older, and we just didn't have the heart and energy to keep being in the uncertain world of dealing with the courts and department decisions.

Lila was not what we had expected. To try to get more information and make a plan as a family, we insisted that the social worker bring her to our home so we could meet before we made a decision. She was foster to adopt. The placement request said, "Eight year old girl needs immediate placement in adoptive home." You would think that would be pretty clear. It really wasn't; her social worker lied.

Since we had had so many bad experiences we were trying to be very cautious. We invited Lila and her social worker to dinner. She put on a good show that night pretending that she was super sweet like she was an angel, but the key word here is "pretend". We learned later that things from the beginning were not as they had been presented; but I get ahead of myself here. After a lot of phone calls with the social worker and family discussions about having her we said, "Yes". The "we" were actually Mom and Dad, I wasn't so sure but went along because well... I had to. I'm the kid in this picture. She moved in just before Halloween and immediately her true nature started to be seen.

As the holidays were coming, Kylee became anxious to go home so in true social worker ways they planned a meeting. Mom attended with Kylee and a lot of other adults but Dad couldn't go to this one. Kylee had an attorney and she told him that she wanted to go home, so the Department agreed and a plan for her to go home was made. Once Kylee had confirmation that she would be going home in about a month, she just got super bratty and stopped behaving, even for my parents. She started doing things that she shouldn't be doing, and behaving inappropriately, like not coming home afterschool and "disappearing" for hours without permission. This behavior was not a shock for me, but it was for my parents and it created a lot of extra stress. She finally left on November 12th. This goodbye was easy because Mom and Dad helped her take her things to her home and said goodbye. And we were back to just Lila.

Lila wasted no time trying to be in charge in our home. She was a rough-looking, chubby Mexican-American girl with a raspy voice. She started out by refusing to eat what Mom cooked. Now I am a picky eater, so Mom is pretty good at making stuff that is tasty to even me, but Lila wanted Hostess cakes for breakfast and fast food all the time. The battles began, because Mom is very stubborn. If she wants some healthy food, like carrots, yogurt, corn, cheese or some protein product to be eaten, she will wait you out. Lila thought she could outwait my mom, which was not going to happen. Her reactions to limits and boundaries were right out of some, "kid with behavior problems" book and so Mom followed the, "how to positively discipline your hard to learn behavior problem kid" book. I don't really think these are titles, but it really tells what it was like to watch the two of them.

Lauren-Brooks Wilson

Unlike the other kids who came with nothing, Lila came with tons of stuff... everything she had gotten since she came into foster care. There was loads of it. Her clothes were a problem by typical eight year old standards. They were very "hoochy" and too grown-up looking with sparkles, glitter and belly showing shirts that were mostly too tight. Mom had to step in and get her some things that didn't make her stick out so badly in a bad way; she already had friendship issues. I was just thankful that I didn't have to share a room or even a floor in the house with her because she was a mess and kept her room even messier. Mom worked with her on taking showers. When Lila got frustrated with the expectation that she needed to be clean, Mom solved it by signing us up for swimming classes, since she didn't know how to swim. In fact, none of the kids who lived in our home knew how to do any of the "kid basics" like swim, bike ride, or skate; we taught them all. Because we were going to the pool, Lila had to shower and put on lotion afterwards. Mom had to brush her teeth for her because she didn't want to do it and she had a lot of cavities before. With Mom's help she didn't get any new ones, and even fixed some from before by taking care of herself.

Just Out of Reach

Although I was cautious about being a sister to Lila, I was still going to try to be her friend. I know that every kid in foster care has a tough life and could use one. Now that it was just the two of us kids in the home I was thinking that playing with someone is better than no one, right? This didn't work out, in every way I tried. At home I tried to play with her and my toys or even her toys but she was so stubborn and bossy we couldn't actually play. She was too busy telling me how wrong I was playing and setting up rules. Up in my room she would break things that were mine and then sarcastically apologize; she even broke my bed! Sometimes she just made up stuff to tell Mom about me that wasn't even true and didn't happen. I would stand there hearing what she was saying and couldn't believe my ears. Lies to my mom about me??? I just kept thinking, why would she do this if she wanted to have a family? Here we were offering to keep her and she was wrecking it. She even was creepy "girlfriend" with Oliver. That was just gross, since he is like my brother. She obviously had some kind of crush on him but then started saying inappropriate things about him and me, telling Oliver lies about me to turn him against me. Thankfully, Oliver and I are so close that he didn't fall for it; but he also didn't want to play with her much. As all these situations were happening something became clear to even me. The social workers don't write the truth on the placement packet papers because nothing said that she was a friend stealer, liar, messy, bully. Truthfully that paper must not have said much. It seems easy to use flowery language to disguise the truth.

You might wonder the reason I know that the social worker lied. Well after she moved in, about a week later, a visitation transporter showed up at our door. She was hired by the social worker to take Lila to visits with her mom. These visits had been going on for a long time, but the social worker didn't tell us anything about them even happening. The visit person told us that she was "on track to reunify" with her mom in early spring. See, that made no sense to us since she was placed in our home for adoption. WELL WHICH ONE WAS IT? When we asked the social worker that question she didn't have anything to say about it. It also became clear why Lila didn't want to follow our rules or invest much into making living at our home work out. She knew she wasn't staying. And even if it wasn't for certain at that time, it was obvious that was what she wanted. I guess just like every foster kid, she wanted to go home if she could.

Just Out of Reach

Even though she moved to our home in Seattle she continued to go to a school down in Renton. It didn't surprise me to find out that no one was her friend and she had temper tantrums at school. She told me that she stabbed a kid with a pencil and swore at teachers and was just horrible. My parents worked with her, and the school to try to make these days better. She actually started to learn and do her homework just like a regular kid. This took a lot of time each night but I was glad she was doing better at school. A taxi showed up every morning to take her to school, and after school she was driven by taxi again to my afterschool program so that Mom and Dad could pick us up at the same time. It was weird because in our cars she had to ride in a car seat, but in a taxi she didn't? It was also dangerous at times because she had these older men for drivers, and they didn't always take her to the right place. Even though I wasn't very fond of her, I didn't want her getting hurt on the way to my program so until she showed up I was worried, at least in the beginning.

Lauren-Brooks Wilson

I thought because we were "family and sisters" at home that when she got to afterschool program we would get along and play. At first I didn't mind her coming to my programs because we played together okay and she was a little shy in new situations. But I learned later that she was more or less scoping out the scene and was not really shy. Once she settled in things started to change for me. Everyone seemed to love Lila and talk about how great and cool and funny and stylish she was. People who were my friends were being turned against me by her and she was rubbing it in my face, secretly telling me that she was better than me. She also would break the "family code" and tell private stories about me to other people that were embarrassing. These are the things that as a family you can laugh about, but certainly would not want everyone in the school knowing. She had the information and therefore she had the power to humiliate me whenever she wanted.

Just Out of Reach

CHAPTER FIVE

Numbers: 5 & 6
Maybe This Time

Not that we were looking for another kid, but then came Rose, an unplanned placement with no information or notice. I guess we had learned from all the rest that even if there is information it might not be true, so why bother. Mom brought her home on November 22nd and that is when I learned she was coming. I loved her from the first night she came. Her room was across from mine where Kylee had lived, and it felt right to have a sister over there since Angie and Kylee were gone. She was a good girl. Over time we learned that she just made bad decisions at bad times. The plan was for her to live with us for the weekend and through Thanksgiving because she didn't have anywhere else to go and no more family who could have her. She was actually legally free because her parents were in jail for doing bad things and she needed a family to take care of her. By the time Monday came we were all hooked on each other. So Mom and Dad told the social worker that if she wanted to stay with us, we would love to have her. She hadn't been in school yet this year and it was already December so mom signed her up and things were going along so smoothly. We started over again getting to know someone new. Lila had been in our home for about a month and seemed to be in the way of me and Rose all the time. Since Rose was older we got along well and left Lila to be the third wheel. I was glad to have an older sister again and one that seemed to want to be with us.

    Before we knew it a month had passed and things were going so well. At Christmas we decorated the house together, Dad, Mom, Lila, Rose and me. I still missed Angie and Cooper a lot since it was just two Christmas' ago when we had to say goodbye to Angie and one since Cooper. Mom sometimes calls these "sad anniversaries". We put the tree in the corner of the living room, our stockings were hanging from the mantel, and the house looked beautiful. The only thing that didn't look too pretty was my dad's new haircut; for some reason he decided to almost shave his head. Wow. I had never seen him look like that in my whole life. The nice thing about bad haircuts is that they are temporary and his hair eventually grew back. Although Dad's bad haircut was quite remarkable, the most important thing that year was our family gift to Rose; we asked her to stay forever. Before this Mom and Dad had to get permission from the social worker to ask her if she wanted to be adopted by us. Her parents' rights were terminated (another big social worker word) which left her an orphan of Washington. I guess the things her parents did to her were so bad they both had to go to jail forever. So once we had permission to ask Mom and Dad bought a beautiful necklace for her and when she opened it we asked if she wanted to stay as our child. I loved her and was letting my heart open up again despite the horrible things that Lila was doing every day.

      Rose said, "Yes."

Just Out of Reach

We were all so happy. By this time Lila knew that she was going home to her mom's to live. It seemed to me that she would have been happy for us and Rose since she was getting her mom back, but instead she was jealous. She worried that her mom would mess up again and she would not have a good family to come to if moving home didn't work out. Watching us fall in love with Rose must have been hard for her because we could have been her family if she hadn't been going home and been so mean.

The taxi rides taking Lila to school and daycare were becoming more challenging by the time Christmas came so a decision was made to move her to my school. She had also learned how to be more of a kid at school and do her work so academically she was ready for the challenge. By this time it was clear that her mom was going to have her back in her home and if she moved to my school, she could move home without changing schools again. So the decision was made by the social worker, schools and my parents to make the change in February. This was not my plan at all. Once she actually moved to my school it made a BIG conflict because when my parents weren't around, she bullied me even more. Yea, sure laugh at me; she was eight and I was nine. I even laughed at myself when I finally figured it out. She always seemed to know when an adult was around or not watching. The lunch room, playground, and hallways became torturous for me because I could never predict what she would do next. We were not in the same class because I was in fourth grade and she was in third, but it seemed like she was everywhere, and if it wasn't her then it was someone she had enlisted to be on her side to torture me. Getting my parents to believe all the things that were going on was hard, and I was feeling like the crazy one. I persisted and kept telling Mom and Dad about this and they did try to get some protection. But because Lila was so charming and funny people couldn't, or didn't, want to believe how this was hurting me. Even the afterschool staff, who had known me for years, were not supporting me through this. Poor foster kids. That sympathy seemed ridiculous, because she is just a person too and so am I.

One time at the aftercare program I was laying down on a bench and one of the counselors said, "Are you waiting for your prince to wake you?"

Just Out of Reach

I told him, "Oh yes. Definitely." To play into the make believe game we had been playing.

Lila came over and had to butt in. She declared loudly, "Here let me go get a boy to kiss you awake."

And then she went to get a boy! I couldn't tell when she said it that she actually meant it. But there she was going over to a five year friend of mine and asking the boy to kiss me. Thankfully, he said "NO". I was glad, but mad at Lila for the embarrassment. I got up and told her that her actions were unacceptable. While I was headed to go get my backpack, Lila decided that me telling what she did wrong was not acceptable. So guess what she did? She yelled out a whole bunch of names. They were all boys I knew. After she was done yelling out name she said, "Those are all of Lauren's crushes!" and she started laughing hysterically. I got really upset. I just walked away from it all, fuming and nearly in tears.

But no... she wasn't finished yet. I had walked over to my friend and since I trusted him, I told him what had happened. While I was doing that Lila came over for the ultimate humiliation. She came up to us while I was still talking and I told her, "Go away." She just started circling around me and my friend. Finally, once no adults were watching and she knew I couldn't stand it anymore she pushed him and I together like we were kissing. Every one heard the commotion and looked over and by that time Lila had run off to make it look like she had nothing to do with it. None of the counselors believed me even with my friend backing up my story. *Lila was <u>too</u> good to do that,*" was what they said. But once my mom saw me so sad and so down she knew something was wrong. Lila got busted, and so did the counselors that didn't believe me. After that Mom and Dad started picking me up from school early so I didn't have to spend so much time with her. It was clear that she was not going to stay in our home. We just needed to get through these last few months until she moved back with her mom.

In January things seemed a little off with Rose. We were worried about her. Things just had been going so great, and we didn't want it to change. My dad found her diary and he read some of it. Apparently it was like she was a whole different person on paper. Not sweet or cute or truthful. It was horrible. My parents were shocked. She was a whole different person living one life in our world and a totally separate one on paper. My parents started having conversations with her in the office for privacy since Lila and I were always around and listening in. Because I am a kid I thought they were having secret discussions about me. In the end I learned that wasn't the case. They were trying to let Rose know that she could be honest and that we would help her through her thoughts or feelings. But she continued to sneak around and it only got worse. She wouldn't share any of her new "friends" names or phone numbers with my mom. She was taking more time after school to get home and seemed to be "missing" for up to an hour at times.

Then….one day Rose came home from school, packed a bag and left. The reason? There was a dance party in the city and for her to go Mom had to have the phone number of the boy she was going with and some details for safety. Rose didn't give Mom the number, but she was determined to go to the dance. So in her mind she gave up our family to hang out for one night. That day Dad got home first, he called Mom when he found the note. Our family was devastated. Then Mom, me, and Lila got home. Yes, Lila was still living with us. Here we were again losing the one we wanted to keep but had the one we weren't keeping and didn't want. I was crying. It was February and by then we knew Lila wasn't staying, but she made it all about herself trying to be so dramatic and hog the attention that should have been focused on getting Rose back. She kept saying "Why aren't my feelings important?! She was going to be my forever sister too!!!!! I loved her more than all of you!!!!" Those were her exact words. She started crying really loud to get attention, but all she got was told to "Go to your room if you want to have a fit." Mom and Dad were serious about finding Rose and were not going to put up with Lila's drama and distractions. That got her to stop.

    I was shocked at how Lila was behaving. Really, Rose was not going to be her sister at all; Lila was leaving. We weren't denying Lila's feelings. We knew she enjoyed Rose, we all did. But she was trying to take the attention away from the problem at hand, and it wasn't helping. Dad took the car to look for Rose, and Mom called the police and social worker and told them she had run away. We just sat and waited. Waiting for anything. Imagine, having so many people leave and you're only nine. I'd been hurt a lot and this was the final straw. I wanted her to walk back in the door and explain that she had made a mistake but she was back now for good. That didn't happen and the weekend wore on without her; all of us worrying. One of the kids my mom works with happened to be there at the party that Rose went to. She knew that Mom wouldn't have wanted Rose there, so she brought Rose to her home and kept her safe all weekend.

Mom got the call three days later from that kid she knew. She told her that Rose was at the Starbucks near our home. Mom went with the police to get her because by that time she had a run report with the police and warrant with the court to be taken to see the judge when she was found. The social worked placed Rose in another foster home. We asked to have some therapy with Rose to figure out what happened and make it right so she could return, but the social worker just ignored our requests. Rose went on to live in a lot of different foster homes and only stayed for about three months each time. She would get a "boyfriend" and then run away. Mom was able to see her after she left because she is a social worker too. So at least I would know she was safe or when she was around. I could have visited her but was a little scared of my feelings seeing her out there with another family so I never took my mom up on the offer.

    Then it was just Lila.

    I use to feel bad for Lila because of what happened to her. But after that final situation at school I felt nothing. She was just a lonely, selfish, rude person. By this time I think I was getting tired of trying so hard to help and teach and be a good sister and never having it work out. I was pulled out of the afterschool program because it wasn't safe for me anymore and my mom and dad got a therapist for me to talk to because I was feeling so sick all the time. I know my mom and dad wanted to protect me so they told the Department that Lila needed to move. At that point everyone was saying that the plan was for her to go back to her mom's home to live. We had said that she needed to be moved by the beginning of April, but I guess her mom wasn't ready for her to come back so they told us we needed to keep her until May. Why do they get to do that, the social workers? It's my life and our family. It should be our choice! My life with her in it just got worse and worse. Lila and the girl from school who had been bulling me since third grade were both bullying me. Of course they became fast friends! I hated Lila and what she did to me but we kept our promise and she stayed until May. She had no right to stay, but she did.

Mom and Dad did their best to keep her away from me, but the last straw came when my mom was picking me up from school and couldn't find my backpack in the hallway. Lila had been nearby, so I guess my mom was skeptical about what she might have done to me this time. Until her arrival I had never had problems with my belongings or getting through the day feeling so bad. We searched for about ten minutes and finally found my pack, in the boy's bathroom on the toilet. GROSS!!! My mom called her out in front of everyone about how inappropriate it was for her to touch my backpack. She denied it with her lying smile on her face, and of course everyone believed her instead. That was Mom's last straw; Mom called the social worker and demanded that Lila leave. She finally left our house the next day. Mom had packed and moved most of her things earlier that month to her mom's apartment knowing she was moving soon, so all she had left was a duffle bag.

BUT, I wasn't rid of her since there were still two months of school left and she was in the class across the hall. I never went back to the afterschool program for the remainder of the year. I was going to homework club twice a week, but then out of the blue she showed up there too, so Mom and Dad pulled me out of that program as well. This was hard for us all because someone had to be there to get me each day afterschool and both my parents worked. All this shuffling around was so inconvenient and added stress to our lives, but I knew that my parents were doing everything they could to keep me safe. This had been my school and my home; everything was invaded by her and changed forever. At the end of that school year I never went back, Mom and Dad were tired of the school and daycare failing to protect me.

When summer came I was so glad. Since Lila was our last kid to leave and we were not going to do this to our family anymore, we finally got to breathe and figure out what we had left of us. Of all the kids who have come and gone, Rose has been the only one that I can continue to see. She shows up now and then, without warning or a plan, spends a day or dinner with us. Now she's going on 17 and we just continue to tell her that she has a safe home with us, if she ever wants to come back.

After Lila left we closed our home. We don't have a foster/adopt license anymore – so the court has made a special order that allows us to have Rose at our home without anyone being in trouble. I'm glad that her most recent social worker (she has had five since she lived with us) was willing to do that for her… and us.

Lauren-Brooks Wilson

CHAPTER SIX

Number: Just me
The Other Side of it All

And now? Now my family has exchange students. You see we built this big home for a big family that never came to be. All the empty rooms were a sad reminder of what isn't, so we fill them up with international students and we are doing ok. I have moved to another school and there are no foster kids around to take all the attention or hurt me. The experience of having foster kids and never being able to adopt any of them during my childhood has kind of traumatized me and I will never forget it. We have finished the remodel of our house and have little breaks from all the exchange students but we're still a family and we will always stick together through all the fights to all the love. Our future plan is to sell the house and pack up these memories the best we can. We will start fresh, just the three of us.

My name is Lauren and this was my life. I've been through all of this stuff and it will forever be a part of me. It will always be somewhere up in my head. It was important for me to write this book because I wanted people to know my story and maybe make good choices for their own family if they are thinking about becoming a foster or adoptive family. This is my way of letting out the memories of that time so I don't keep it all inside forever. I will never forget all the love they gave, hard times that were created by their presence and absence, and hurt that is slowly healing.

Thanks and Appreciation

My parents for their love and support, Christine Pinto and Erin Adams for their edits to help me tell my story. Thanks to Henry and Laina for their help with the hands on the cover.

Made in the USA
San Bernardino, CA
11 January 2014